WORKPLACE CHANGES IN PROGRESS

Self-Directed Work Teams

By

Tom H. Washington

ISBN: 978-1-4107-7793-5 (sc)
ISBN: 978-1-4107-7794-2 (hc)
ISBN: 978-1-4107-7792-8 (e)

Print information available on the last page.

This book is printed on acid-free paper.

1stBooks - rev. 05/17/2021

Acknowledgment

Even though there are many to whom I owe a sense of gratitude, I am grateful to Dr. Lee Holtzen at Concordia University Seward, Nebraska. His sensitivity and awesome enthusiasm to the Action Research Program are deeply appreciated. Also, heartfelt thanks to Fred Plantevin, Terry L. Sprieck and Larry Zach three of Becton Dickinson's BDPS and BDMS managers for their unwavering support. Without their support throughout the research, this book would not have been written in this form.

About the Book:

Introduction

Self-directed work teams are gaining popularity as an alternative to traditional work designs. This study attempts to address what is the "driving force" behind the installation of self-directed work teams. What stage have self-directed work teams developed within the various organizations? How is the self-directed work teams "governed"? What are the steps followed in installing self-directed work teams? What problems are encountered at each step of the installation? What solutions are used to solve the problems encountered, and what would be the results (effects on performance impact on supervisors, productivity, costs, absenteeism, and job satisfaction) from implementing self-directed work teams?

The study used an organizational guiding behavior survey. The survey was administered to workers on December 16, 1998, at Becton-Dickinson when 56 surveys documents were distributed to each department #242 work cells and #272 non-work cells in Columbus, Nebraska, and all returned completed.

This project incorporate, a study of current trends in self-directed work teams programs, as they apply to the management-associates relations process. This study shows how managers are becoming more involved with their work force, to empower associates to make their own decisions, decrease associates job dissatisfaction, and allow for flatter organizational charts.

In today's work environment, there is a need to change the way management and the associates communicate. The traditional way that management communicates with the associates is by telling them what to do, and how to do their job. In years past the traditional democratic style of management was effective, but in today's work environment requires a flatter coaching style of management.

Based on the project study one objective was established, to flattening management hierarchy and create a coaching atmosphere instead of telling. The self-directed work team transformation in today's workplace is in the form of how managers are becoming more like mentors and coaches when communicating with associates.

Tom H. Washington

Summer 2000

Table of Contents

CHAPTER 1

Workplace Changes In Progress

The Becton Dickinson Corporation was established in Columbus, Nebraska, on October 12, 1949. The plant is one of several in the United States, and specializes in the production of a medical device. The average current daily output of Becton-Dickinson is several million medical devices per week in the Columbus plant.

Columbus has a population of about 19,500, and Becton Dickinson must compete with several other major corporations as it seeks to hire staff for its plant. A large number of laborers is available from surrounding small towns, but those seeking work have a number of options, due to the Columbus industry's growth and the low unemployment rate in recent years.

Becton-Dickinson's Columbus plant normally employs 700 workers on the production line, with another 200 associates involved as support staff and management. As of September 30, 1997, the workforce included 360 (40%) male and 540 (60%) female associates. The distribution for workers in management was 125 (63%) male and 75 (37%) female associates.

For several decades, Becton-Dickinson organized its management according to a pattern typical of similar factories in the Midwest. A supervisor was placed in charge of a department to supervise 60-70 production line workers. The supervisor was directly responsible to the production manager. The associates on the line were encouraged to provide input to the supervisor by means of written suggestions.

In an effort to provide a stronger sense of ownership by production associates, some experimentation has been introduced, with the formation of work cells and self-directed work teams, including 15-20 associates, none of whom is designated as a "coordinator" or "supervisor." As of September 30, 1997, management had in place three such work cells, organized around the stated purposes of the work cell organization including the following:

- Associates on the line should develop a stronger sense of ownership in tasks common to all associates in the group
- Associates on the line should find it easier to suggest ways in which their segment of production can become more efficient, and to implement such strategies on a limited basis, allowing all members of the work cell to make observations concerning the efficiency of any new strategy

Management made the decision five years ago to implement work cells in the Columbus plant. From management's point of view, work cells were the direction to go in optimizing work relations, quality improvement, cost reduction and ownership. A change in work relations reinforces the ability of associates to have mutual respect, openness and trust for fellow associates. Quality improvement at each process operation gives the associates an understanding that quality means business, and the absence of quality means loss of business. Associates come up with cost reduction ideas and understand the need to compete on a worldwide basis. A change in attitude helps associates look at things differently, and gives them a new perspective and a change in paradigm, and ultimately helps them come up with new ideas and to think outside the box.

Self-directed work teams will help associates make decisions at the lowest level. Making decisions at the lowest level means: having information available, knowing the schedules, overall expectations, and due dates; if this is implemented at the associate level, management hierarchy can be reduced. Decision-making at the lowest level is a time and money saver for the associates and the company.

Conversely to all of the previous stated benefits that self-directed work teams provide, there are disadvantages to the process. There is some resistance to the idea and to the process. It is not clear whether resistance is due to a lack of understanding or a lack of training. Sometimes inadequate training can be a major obstacle for individuals without the necessary training in the work cells concept.

Are associates reluctant to change? Maybe associates are comfortable in their present environment and they are unwilling to accept changes. Sometimes associates feel they have been doing things this way for many years, so why change? For some associates, the least thought of change gives them a feeling that something will be taken away from them, or that management does not care anymore. Sometimes associates feels they will have to do more work for less pay.

Lastly, has management really bought into the idea of self-directed work teams? These questions need to be answered in order to build on a solid foundation for positive results in implementing self-directed work teams.

Answers to these questions will be sought by way of a survey. Surveying the existing work cells should provide some insights as to why there is resistance to the self-directed work team concept. Some of the questions to be surveyed include such things as:

- What does a self-directed work team mean to you?

- What do you like about a self-directed work team?

- What do you dislike about a self-directed work team?

- If you could change one thing about your team, what would it be?

- Do you think that you get the support needed from management?

The use of the survey will give some answers to important questions about the pros and cons of self-directed work teams. It is expected that the survey will bring to the surface some deep personal feelings in regards to the work cells.

The goal of this book is to explore the advantages of a self-directed work team. In writing this book, I have used numerous books and authors for research material. Several books have been written on self-directed work teams that show a rich history of successful companies, and my survey of these companies will be an integral part of this book.

CHAPTER 2

TEXT REVIEW

The increase in both U.S. and global competition has required firms to become innovative, and incorporate ideas that increase employee motivation and productivity while decreasing costs. One method that has had great success is the use of self-managed work teams. William Passmore reports in his article "Developing Self-Managing Work Teams: An Approach to Successful Integration" that self-managed work teams are increasing in their popularity, and many U.S. firms are using different forms of these teams to help increase production, streamline the organizational process, and maintain a higher level of commitment and motivation among employees.

The concept of self-managed work teams originated from the use of action teams. While both types of teams are good at increasing employee confidence and development on an individual basis, action teams are formed to solve a specific problem within the company, whereas self-managed teams are given the task of undertaking full responsibility for the entire function of the company. In the article "TQM and the Team Solution," John E. Glorioso uses the example of a manufacturing company which has to make room for the introduction of new technologically advanced equipment, to show where an action team would be used effectively. He also gives examples of functions self-managed teams might be assigned to control. Some of these include coordinating training, setting up schedules, budget responsibilities, disciplinary problems and hiring practices, or any combination of these for a larger project.

Self-managed teams have become commonplace in many organizations, but they are not always the right choice. William Passmore believes the organization must determine if self-management is the proper choice for an organization to reach its goals of increased market competitiveness. He states that there are three basic considerations in the decision to use self-managed teams.

The first consideration is how competitive the market actually is for the product or service being delivered. If the market is extremely competitive, like the high-tech industry, then self-managed teams have documented successes. Other industries, such as utilities that are not experiencing a strong competitive force, find that self-management and the team concept are not beneficial, especially considering the time and economic investment required.

The second consideration deals with the firm's organizational values and goals. Successful teams are found in organizations that believe in true empowerment and equality in the work force. Companies that rely heavily on an autocratic system will have a difficult time gaining employee acceptance for such an operation. Employees in this type of organization know there is no true empowerment and do not feel the need to put forth the extra effort needed to make a self-managed team successful.

The last consideration deals with the capabilities of the employees and the technology used. This is seen in companies that have highly specialized production equipment and use specifically selected individuals to operate it, making it difficult to form a team.

Once the decision is made that a self-managed work team would be beneficial to the company, the real work begins. It is not an easy process to develop a team. A great deal of time, patience, and resources are required to make a successful beginning. Many times organizations rush into the formation of these teams, expecting results in unrealistically short time periods. This only leads to frustration, both on the part of upper management and the employees involved in the process.

One important part of the formation of a self-managed team, according to Dean Elmuti in his article "Sustaining High Performance Through Self-Managed

Work Teams," is the link it has with empowerment.

Elmuti states that allowing the employees the ability to

make decisions that impact them is crucial to the

success of the team. Empowerment is a good catch-

phrase from the 90s, but it must be practiced, not just

preached, in order to obtain increases in individual

motivation and productivity.

Along with empowering the employees, it is also

essential to have adequate time to plan the process

and to deal with issues that are to be covered by the

team. According to Glorioso, the planning process

must start with management's addressing the issues

that are necessary for a smooth transition from

autocratic management to self-management.

Some of these issues include the need for

managers to accept worker decision-making, the need

for open lines of communication and how they are to

be set up to help the team progress, and serious evaluation of the time and money needed to properly invest in the project. Glorioso also points out that it is imperative to have management committed to supporting the project with disclosure of pertinent information the team will need.

For companies trying to form self-managed teams, Glorioso recommends a transition stage from action teams to self-managed teams. As mentioned before, action teams are used in more specific problem-solving areas. It is thought that the training, level of responsibility, and decision-making granted to an action team will provide a good stepping stone for self-managed teams to get started. Once the fundamental groundwork has been mastered, the self-managed team can be used more efficiently for larger-scope projects.

Passmore discusses the development time needed for teams to evolve into self-management teams, and how it varies from one company to the next, but usually falls within a range of 18 months to three years.

To illustrate the process, Passmore uses Intel to give a picture of how involved the process can be and how much time is actually involved.

Intel is considered a high-technology company, heavily involved in the development, production, and distribution of computer chips, so it was a good candidate for the use of self-managed teams. Intel knew that their plan had to involve the team's ability to control all the tasks required in order to be successful. They decided to carefully stage the development of the control teams so that once they started they could achieve production goals quickly.

The developers of the team projected a period of 24-36 months for the teams to be fully mature in their decision-making capabilities. This time period was not conducive to the speed necessary to remain competitive in the market. The developers needed to shorten this interval to the "intercept" or milestone set to meet the competition.

Intel decided to rearrange the "ramp" phase, which is the time between starting the teams and meeting the intercept milestone. They were originally going to phase out traditional management roles while increasing production levels and working toward increased delivery and customer service. Instead, the developers retained the supervisors as external support through the ramp and intercept phases. These individuals, because of their knowledge level, aided as leaders and facilitators until the teams were able to absorb some of the responsibility themselves.

The teams eventually took on the operations involving technology, inventory control, quality, and training in areas most needed to obtain production goals. The team did not address some other specialty areas until they were past the intercept point. This helped to avoid stress overload relating to the new changes.

This development process with the ramp and intercept phases is one of the more involved transition processes. Elmuti cites Eastman Kodak Company as another example of how self-managed teams have been successful. The difference between Kodak and Intel is that Kodak did not use developers in their transition process. Instead, employees were encouraged to form groups to initially gather ideas that would help them become more self-reliant in order to increase productivity.

In this example, management also remained in the picture to support and reinforce decisions made by the work teams. Elmuti notes that open lines of communication and an open-minded atmosphere toward new ideas were essential elements in the success of the self-managed team process.

In the book *Business without Bosses,* authors Charles C. Manz and Henry P. Simms discuss how teams evolve and are able to take on greater responsibility to produce remarkable quality and product innovation, and to implement good business decisions. The authors refer to these more mature teams as "super-teams," and state the many benefits of incorporating these teams. As mentioned earlier, some of these benefits include a reduction in management/employee conflict, a more motivated and productive work force, an increase in the range of ownership by employees, and an increase in productivity.

These benefits have been cited by many companies, and the use of self-managed teams is becoming the popular choice of others who are in need of a program that will help retain or regain a competitive edge in today's market. While these rewards are attractive, companies must be prepared for the tremendous amount of effort and commitment needed to properly introduce and implement self-managed teams in their work force.

Successfully integrating new business processes into a corporation is no small feat. In fact, most reengineering failures are really failures in implementation. A concurrent culture change process is synergistic with reengineering, and will improve the chances for successful implementation of newly reengineered systems and processes.

This synergy works because the successful implementation of reengineering requires a shift from a functional (vertical) orientation to a process (horizontal) orientation, where people in the organization must now focus on common objectives across traditional departmental boundaries. The practical problem with the implementation of such a shift is that, to be successful, employees must know each other, trust each other, and learn to openly communicate with those in other departments. In many traditional vertically structured organizations, such cross-departmental cooperation and communication has not been the case and, in many cultures, it was not encouraged either. Thus, a culture of mistrust and weak horizontal communications is heavily ingrained in informal systems and strong behavioral norms that hinder reengineering (self-management).

A culture change process brings about just such broad, cross-functional interactions, especially when culture change training and cross-functional team-building are combined with changes in the daily business behaviors, and reinforced through company-wide communications and people actively coaching one another. Culture change is a necessary platform for reengineering success (self-management).

In order to change behaviors and reshape a culture, a process is needed to unfreeze these locked-in beliefs and habitual behaviors. The process of unfreezing organizational beliefs is very different from those which are used for the development of organizational structure in a strategic plan. Changing mindset requires a different learning methodology and process, one that is often less familiar and therefore initially somewhat less comfortable for organizations in need of change.

This creates another rule of culture change not stated earlier, and that is that a culture will tend to reject and resist what it most needs to help change it.

For example, cultures that are very rational and analytical will want to use only rational and analytical processes to change the culture. Since human behaviors and beliefs are not rational and logical, that's a recipe for failure.

The successful implementation of a change in corporate culture requires a series of specially designed non-traditional interventions. Research into behavior change has shown that there are two primary ways to modify behavior. One is traditional "behavior modification" through reinforcement activities such as rewards and performance appraisals. While reinforcement is one element of culture change, by itself it is not powerful enough to shift an entrenched culture. Behavior modification, including performance appraisal, is far too slow in changing behaviors; it is often too indirect and tends to be externally, not internally, driven.

Research has shown that people develop a powerful internal drive to change only after they have had an emotionally powerful "transformational experience." Most of us probably know of at least one business executive who has either had a heart attack or bypass surgery, and the experience was so profound that they wound up changing their ways. The workaholic, cheeseburger-eating person you once knew is now a dedicated runner and somewhat of an evangelist about fat-free foods! This is the result of a life changed due to a "transformational" experience. Similar changes are seen following a divorce, the death of a loved one, or the birth of a child. Emotional experience often causes one to step back from their old life patterns, reexamine their beliefs and behaviors, and become committed to rebuilding a life with more balanced meaning than before. The significant emotional event creates an "unfreezing" and "openness for change" that didn't exist before, even though the dangers of lack of exercise, poor eating habits, poor communication at home, etc. are well known.

Similarly, to shift corporate culture, the employees of the organization must have a significant transformational experience that causes them to develop an openness for change that did not exist before. While this experience can come from such business events as a near bankruptcy, a takeover attempt, a precipitous drop in sales or income, fear of job loss, or competitive attack on their core business, these events are external and often create a reactive, fear-driven response. A positive proactive transformational experience can be created through the implementation of specially designed "culture change" seminars for managers and employees. Once employees truly "feel" the need for change, and experience how much better their business (and personal) life can be in a new, high-performance culture, there is a quantum leap in commitment to the change process.

Self-managing teams are the most promising and exciting revolution in American companies today.

They may be called self-directed teams, high-performing teams, or employee involvement teams, but whatever they are called, they are proving to be the most productive innovation in American industry in years, and the wave of the future.

A self-managing team is a group of workers that has a high degree of decision-making and problem-solving responsibility and essentially manages itself. It is based on the idea that the people doing the work are the experts in those jobs, and the best way to manage is to empower them to take charge of their own destiny.

The role of management is turned upside down in this new environment. The manager's job is to lead, empower people, and remove roadblocks that get in the way of the team's being able to do its job. The new primary responsibility of the manager is to act as a coach and help teams mature in their development toward self-management.

For team leaders to function effectively in a self-managing team system that is legitimized, they must become skilled in facilitating three critical control functions: directing their fellow team members, monitoring their peers for compliance with the team's directions, and eliminating any behavioral deviance from the team's directions.

These three skills are all items that the traditional supervisor can do relatively easily. However, because of the form of authority that legitimizes control in self-managing teams, the team leader cannot "manage" in a traditional system. The team leader must lead a group of peers, and this leadership must be consistent with the system of control and the form of authority that develops in a self-managing environment. By forming team leadership in teams that are consistent with self-managing teams, the corporation can more effectively teach leaders and organize its existing knowledge about leadership on teams.

Identification allows workers to cope with the demands the organization places on them and, in addition, pushes them to act (to make decisions) in the best interests of the organization.

Self-management teams refer to an organizational structure that requires a heightened level of value-based identification (Barker, 1993a; Sundstrom, De Meuse and Futrell, 1990). Very popular among small to mid-sized companies, the team concept calls for breaking down the traditional tall organizational hierarchy into a flat confederation of self-managing work groups.

Self-managing teams are peer groups of about 10-15 people who assume total responsibility for their area of accountability, whether they work in a service, manufacturing, or information industry. These groups make all the decisions, do all the coordination, and perform all that is required to complete an end-product. Self-managing teams (theoretically) have no first-line supervisors; the team does its own supervising of self and others, thus multiplying the number of potential supervisors. The team hires and disciplines its own members, coordinates directly with other departments for supplies and information, and negotiates with other manufacturing teams to solve production problems and overcome obstacles. Such teams work best in organizations characterized by interdependent tasks, complex processes, sensitivity to deadlines, and the need for rapid change and adaptation.

In a self-managing structure, workers must assume appropriate roles as both team members and organization members. They must accept and work with the premises of both their team and the company. However, in shaping the worker's "organization personality," the team appears to be the key. Researchers have suggested that the team plays a pivotal role in the identification process of self-managing workers. Self-managing teams function in an environment of heightened intensity. Team peer pressure becomes the dominant form of control: instead of one supervisor, the team member now has 10, 12, or more.

Team members expect each other to identify with the team and to behave according to the team's norms and rules. By violating team norms or exhibiting elements of "dis-identification," a team member risks punishment by the team. The offending teammate may be accused of not being a team player or of not being faithful to the "team's personality." This heightened sense of identification creates a powerful force for control in the self-managing environment.

In this environment, the leader's responsibilities for directing differ from the traditional managerial function of giving orders. The team can and should give itself orders based on its negotiated values and normative rules. The team leader's responsibility now becomes one of focusing and persuading. In the early stages of team development, the leader has to understand that the team needs to reach consensus on key values, and the leader should focus the team toward identifying what the team members believe to be the elements of "doing good work on the team." In later stages, the team leader must persuade the team to adopt norms and rules for dealing with recurring decisions or persistent problems, such as how to choose between competing customer demands and how to hold themselves accountable to these rules.

The essential requirement here is that the leader facilitate the team toward establishing parameters for actions. In organizations of diverse members, we learn how to work together by creating an acceptable sense of order out of the chaos of competing goals and desires. This sense of order is a set of behavior parameters, such as value-based norms and rules. Examples of these parameters include the norm that all team members should be at work on time, the norm that the team will always build the "Acme" order first because Acme is the company's best customer, or the norm that the team will hold a 15-minute meeting each morning.

What the leader does here is not to give orders but to direct the team toward discussing and setting these parameters. When the team is discussing and setting parameters, it is, at the same time, reaching a consensus on values and establishing normative rules. If the team has value consensus and a set of normative rules, they can give themselves good orders.

However, the team leader must also face a very serious problem for the team: time management. Time is the biggest enemy of self-managing teams. The hectic pace of today's work environment means that the team will always be pressed for time. Unfortunately, "doing" teamwork demands much time and energy from the team members. In addition, today's competitive business environment does not give time freely. The leader will often be pressured to assume the role of traditional manager and give orders to the team.

The team will find itself being carried away with making rules rather than taking the time to think through the necessity and usefulness of the rules. For example, a team that has a rule that everyone must come to work on time may tire of dealing with a few workers who are consistently tardy and, out of frustration, develop a very rigid draft rule governing tardiness, such as docking workers' pay for being a few minutes late. Taking this path of least resistance will only increase the number of complaints to the human resources department and ultimately degrade the team's performance.

The monitoring function requires that the leader facilitate the team's ability to supervise itself. The team has establishes its own system of checks and balances as a means of monitoring its own work activity. As a start, the leader should ensure that the teams' members reach consensus on their values for self-monitoring and establish a set of norms that pertain to evaluating their own effectiveness.

The team leader may help establish a formula for the team to "confirm" that all the members understand the goals and directions of the team, such as having a few team members brief back the decisions made at a team meeting to the rest of the group. The team leader may facilitate a regular feedback session with senior management and the team to "evaluate" the team performance.

The team leader has to resist the pressure to assume the traditional first-line supervisor role, and senior management has to be supportive. The team leader must keep the team focused on creating and implementing their own systems of monitoring (including confirming and evaluation activities). Keeping the team focused on their need to self-evaluate is the key to achieving this control function.

Self-discipline is the hardest function for the team to perform. The traditional supervisor can discipline errant behavior much more easily than a group of peers. Here, the team leader's key task is to get the team to confront the issue directly. That is, the leader has to persuade the team that they must acknowledge their need to discipline each other from time to time, and that they should reach consensus on a set of appropriate values and behavioral norms for disciplinary situations.

Again, the path of least resistance is for the team to turn over disciplinary cases to the leader, or to adopt a set of draft rules, neither of which works over the long term. The leader's first line of action is to prepare the team to deal with disciplinary situations. The second line of action is to have some training in mediation skills. A team leader can be very effective in playing the role of the "cooler head that prevails" in difficult disciplinary situations.

The team leader must be aware of another critical issue that falls into the realm of deviation elimination. Teams can easily be carried away with creating rational rules. Diverse teams face a natural tendency to create strong systems of rational rules (Barker, 1993), and these rules can be very useful for the team. However, these rational rules make the team vulnerable to the pitfalls of any bureaucracy. The team can get bogged down by its own rules and find itself unable to easily change and adapt to new business situations.

The leader must be able to recognize when the team is becoming bogged down by its rules and when the team environment is becoming oppressive. The team leader must be able to take some type of corrective action. As Hackman and Walton (1986) have suggested, the team periodically needs to review its norms and rules and evaluate how well they are working for the team. Leaders must facilitate this process, even at the expense of short-term productivity. Also, the leader must be able to turn to senior management for help if the team's system of controls appears to be getting out of hand.

The team leader should not forget that eliminating deviation also means dispensing rewards. The leader should focus the team toward establishing its own system of recognizing outstanding behavior, even if senior management does not follow suit. The team needs a systematic mechanism for patting itself on the back.

CHAPTER 3

OPTION ONE - APPLIED DESIGN INTERVENTION

I selected applied design intervention as option number one, because of the number of books written, the amount of research, and the number of businesses that are practicing the method of "self-directed work teams" in the work place. In reading and researching self-directed work teams, I have found that the material available is educational and directional. Some of the authors give clear and concise directions on how to implement reengineering or self-directed work teams.

Some authors point out problems that lead to changes, and some imply that in order to remain competitive, corporations must change the way business is conducted. Some businesses made changes after it was determined that they were in violation of antitrust laws. An example would be AT&T, which discovered that they could not continue with business as usual. Therefore, in order to remain competitive, changes were made.

We will look at some of the suggested changes, in order to have a successful cultural transformation.

Strategic Understanding of Culture Change

Strategic understanding of culture change is the most important first step that helps an organization see the impact of culture on organizational performance. It is useful here to educate management on what culture is, where it comes from, how it affects performance, and the overall process of culture change. It is also important at this initial stage to begin a general discussion about what changes are happening in their industry and why the culture needs to change (Chidress and Senn, 1995).

The Culture Audit

In re-engineering self-directed work teams, bench making, and baseline measure are important as an early part of the process. These activities define the magnitude of the opportunity and establish a starting point for measuring progress. Parallels exist in cultural self-directed work teams as well:

- What is the level of readiness for change?

- How deep are issues of mistrust?

- How aligned is the senior team?

- What are the key cultural barriers to change?

- What cultural and organizational changes are needed to support self-directed work teams?

These and other questions needs to be fully answered and understood before culture change begins.

Begin at the top

This is the most critical phase and builds on the premise that organizations are "shadows of their leaders." For a culture-shift to truly take root, the top management team must become role models of new cultural values and guiding behaviors. This requires introspection and self-assessment on the part of senior management. The CEO and each member of the senior management team must ask them themselves the following:

- What role model do I present to the organization?

- What kind of shadow do I cast?

- Am I, as a member of the senior management team, in alignment with our mission and values?

Communication and teamwork barriers must first be overcome at the top. A clear vision of the new culture must be collectively developed and thoroughly understood at the senior-most level before it can be actively implemented and translated into day-to-day policy and behavior changes necessary to shift a culture.

Conversely, option two, a grant proposal submission would not be a recommended option for my book, because of the submission of a grant proposal to a foundation or an agency for funding. Whereas option one permits an intervention to use existing techniques to improve or alleviate the problem.

Option three: alternative policy decision also would not be a recommended option for my book.

Because option three requires a proposal to change policy. Policy change is not what I am suggesting. I am suggesting a change in the way the business is run, and option one allows for this.

CHAPTER 4

DESCRIPTION OF THE INTERVENTION

This book is presented to help design, educate, train, and implement self-directed work teams. Industries are changing to self-directed work teams at a rapid pace in order to stay competitive. Therefore, self-directed work teams provide a way to cut costs, increase worker ownership and control over their workstations, and improve quality.

Objective One

A self-directed work team is a group of independent people who produce a measurable output for a defined customer. The members share the responsibility for the achievement of customer satisfaction and business objectives of the unit.

They are empowered to plan, control, coordinate, and to pursue their objectives. They also document and continuously seek to improve their own work processes.

The concept of empowerment conveys excitement to some and a threat to others. Many are confused about what it means and uncertain about how to achieve it. Empowerment in the work setting, therefore, involves giving people the means, ability, and/or authority to do something they have not done before.

Objective Two

Empowerment implies a transition of responsibilities and essential activities from supervisor/manager to the team. For a transition to take place there has to be readiness on both sides — a readiness to take on, and a readiness to let go.

Empowerment begins by determining what the team will be responsible for. When the team becomes self-directed, it assumes additional responsibility for planning, controlling, coordinating, and improving the work. In short, the team takes responsibility for managing its own performance.

What areas of its performance does it manage? What are the standards of performance the team is accountable for? How will the team monitor its progress? What planning and coordinating tasks will need to be done? By whom?

Objective Three

- Select leader of work group

- Train new members of work group

- Establish relief and break schedules

- Make specific job assignments within work group

- Make minor equipment and machinery repairs

- Make sure needed production materials are available

- Keep record of hours worked by each group member

- Perform quality control inspections and compile QC data

- Prepare daily log of quantity produced and amount of in-process inventory

- Recommend engineering changes for equipment, process, and product

- Select new members for group

- Dismiss members from group

- Evaluate group members for pay raises

- Conduct safety meetings

- Shut down process/assembly if quality is wrong

- Stop production to solve process or quality problems

- Conduct weekly group meetings

- Review quarterly performance of company, plant, and group

- Discipline group members for absenteeism or tardiness

- Resolve conflicts

- Monitor and correct performance

- Initiate improvements

- Approve time off the job

- Conduct performance reviews

- Be responsible for meeting production goals

- Track performance

- Determine and plan for needed overtime

- Call for maintenance help

- Review production reports

- Schedule and carry out changeovers

- Call engineering when needed

- Attend manager staff meetings

- Solve problems when they arise

- Monitor safety

- Ensure work standards are met

- Set team goals and objectives

- Manage area work activities with a minimum of supervision

- Help plan and coordinate work flow

- Take responsibility for daily production

- Determine procedures for best accomplishing the job

- Call for needed technical support

- Troubleshoot day-to-day operating problems as they arise

- Cross-train each other

- Advise management of problems beyond team's control

- Carry out routine or preventive maintenance

- Maintain safety and housekeeping

- Perform quality inspection

- Seek process improvements continuously

- Coordinate with upstream supplier, downstream customer, and off-shift work teams.

Empowerment of self-directed work teams provides ways to cut cost, shift ownership, maintain control over workstations, and improve quality.

CHAPTER 5

THE EVALUATION PLAN

An Organization Guiding Behavior Survey was used to collect data. The primary focus was on present work cells and non-work cell operations. The purpose for using the behavior survey was to find out if implemented work cells have a behavior advantage over non-work cell operations.

For years, companies have been attempting to measure the attitude of employees (and, by inference, the overall corporation) with attitude and opinion surveys. While these have somewhat useful in recording how people feel about such issues as benefits, supervision, service levels, and quality, as a whole they have been ineffective in providing insight into how to improve employee and overall corporate performance. One of the failings of these "attitude" surveys is that they often depend upon "feelings" at the moment, and thus are subject to the normal ups and downs of human personality and quarterly performance.

The results of opinion surveys can change with the announcement of a restructuring or during a difficult labor negotiation. What is really being measured is how people "feel" about things, not how individuals and teams are functioning. While feelings are useful in gauging performance, they do not really give insight into the root causes of performance shortfalls or customer problems.

Since high-performance behaviors and high-performance teams create results for organizations (and fulfillment for individuals), it is more important to ask about levels of cross-organizational teamwork than about how people feel. It is more important to know if there is a motivation for action and a can-do attitude, than it is to know if people are unhappy about declining medical benefits.

It is believed that a whole new approach to measuring and monitoring organizational and individual performance is needed to provide today's corporations with a more effective set of performance improvement tools. Instead of seeking to measure attitudes, it is suggested to measure "behaviors" of actual performance-related activities. When it comes to measuring culture change, what better behaviors or actions to evaluate than the guiding behaviors that constitute the newly-desired corporate culture?

ORGANIZATIONAL GUIDING BEHAVIORS

SURVEY

The survey is built around the company's shared core values, which are guiding behaviors. A list of 14 specific guiding behaviors was developed. Selected associates will fill out an Organizational Guiding Behaviors survey, rating the degree to which the company is currently displaying these important behaviors during the daily performance of work.

The Organizational Guiding Behaviors Survey provides a "picture" of the culture as it currently exists, measured in terms of the "desired" culture.

The survey consists of 14 essential behavior questions that require rating of outstanding, high, average, and, low. The survey was administered to workers on December 16, 1998, at Becton-Dickinson;

56 surveys were distributed to Departments #242 and #272 Columbus, Nebraska and all 112 were returned completed.

The questions are:

➢ We act in harmony

➢ We do what is right

➢ We always seek to improve

➢ We accept personal responsibility

➢ Leadership is shared

➢ Accountability for work/behavior

➢ Personal integrity (myself)

➢ Integrity of others

➢ Personal growth/learning continuing

➢ Dignity and respect

➢ Caring about other/business

➢ Winning

➢ Empowerment

➢ Teamwork

Work cells are similar to self-directed work teams which take on additional responsibilities that normally would be handled by management. Therefore, there should be a clear distinction between work cells and non-work cell operations with an Organizational Guiding Behavior survey.

ORGANIZATIONAL GUIDING BEHAVIOR SURVEY

In an effort to gain information on present Work Cells and Non-Work Cell Operations, I am soliciting your input on where we are in an Organizational Guiding Behaviors Survey. This survey will give a "picture" of the culture as it currently exists, measured in terms of the elements in the "desired" culture. Please rate the following questions on a scale of **1 - 5,**

1 = Low, 5 = Outstanding, and return to your manager/coordinator.

Thanks,

Tom H. Washington

	Outstanding	High	Average	Low
We act in harmony				
We do what is right				
We always seek to improve				
We accept personal responsibility				
Leadership is Shared				
Accountability for work/Behavior				
Personal Integrity (myself)				
Integrity of others				
Personal Growth/Learning				
Dignity and Respect				
Caring about others/Business				
Winning				
Empowerment				
Teamwork				

Additional Comments Are Welcome:

_____

Chapter 6

SUMMARY OF RESULTS

Results from the Organization Guiding Behavior Survey that was administered to department #272 and #242 at Becton-Dickinson in Columbus, Nebraska. Department #272 was a non-work cell and Department #242 was a work cell.

Figure 6.1 shows an example of the summary data from the Organizational Guiding Behavior Survey in Department #242. The summary lists the score for the category on a scale of 1 to 5. The score for each value is the average of all the scores for the 14 guiding behaviors that define the core values. As you can see, the cell is currently strong. We always seek to improve personal integrity (myself), which indicates that it is self-managed. At the same time, the cell seems weakest in shared leadership, "we act in harmony", "we do what is right," empowerment and teamwork. It seems that personal growth/learning continues. We accept personal responsibility. Accountability for work/behavior, winning, dignity/respect, integrity of others, and caring about others/business was acceptable.

Figure 6.2 shows an example of the summary data from an Organizational Guiding Behavior Survey in Department #272. The summary lists the score for the category on a scale of 1 to 5. The score for each value is the average of all the scores for the 14 guiding behaviors that define the core values. As you can see, the non-work cell is currently strong in "we do what is right", "we always seek to improve," personal integrity (myself) which indicates self-management,

Cells	Median
1. We act in harmony	2.33
2. We do what is right	2.60
3 We always seek to improve	**3.07**
4. We accept personal responsibility	2.89
5. Leadership is shared	2.17
6. Accountability for work / behavior	2.89
7. Personal integrity (myself)	**3.37**
8. Integrity of others	2.76
9. Personal growth / learning continues	2.92
10. Dignity and respect	2.78
11. Caring about others / business	2.75
12. Winning	2.80
13. Empowerment	2.60
14. Teamwork	2.62

Figure 6.1

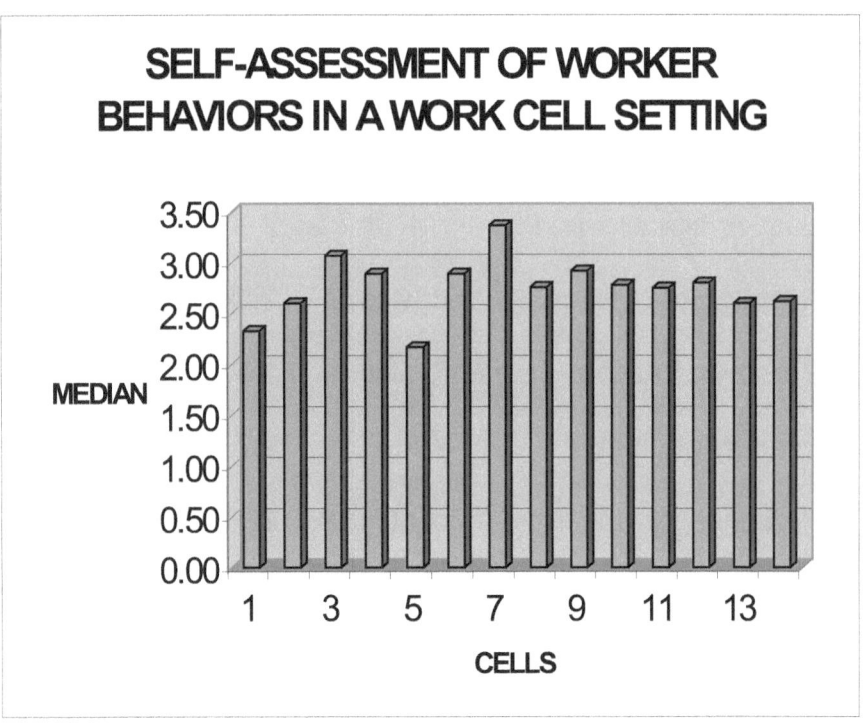

WORK CELLS DEPARTMENT #242

Non-Cells	Median
1. We act in harmony	2.61
2. We do what is right	**3.21**
3. We always seek to improve	**3.24**
4. We accept personal responsibility	2.75
5. Leadership is shared	2.24
6. Accountability for work/behavior	2.49
7. Personal integrity (myself)	**3.54**
8. Integrity of others	**3.17**
9. Personal growth/learning continues	2.98
10. Dignity and respect	**3.10**
11.Caring about others/business	**3.07**
12. Winning	2.85

13. Empowerment   2.59

14. Teamwork   2.87

Figure 6.2

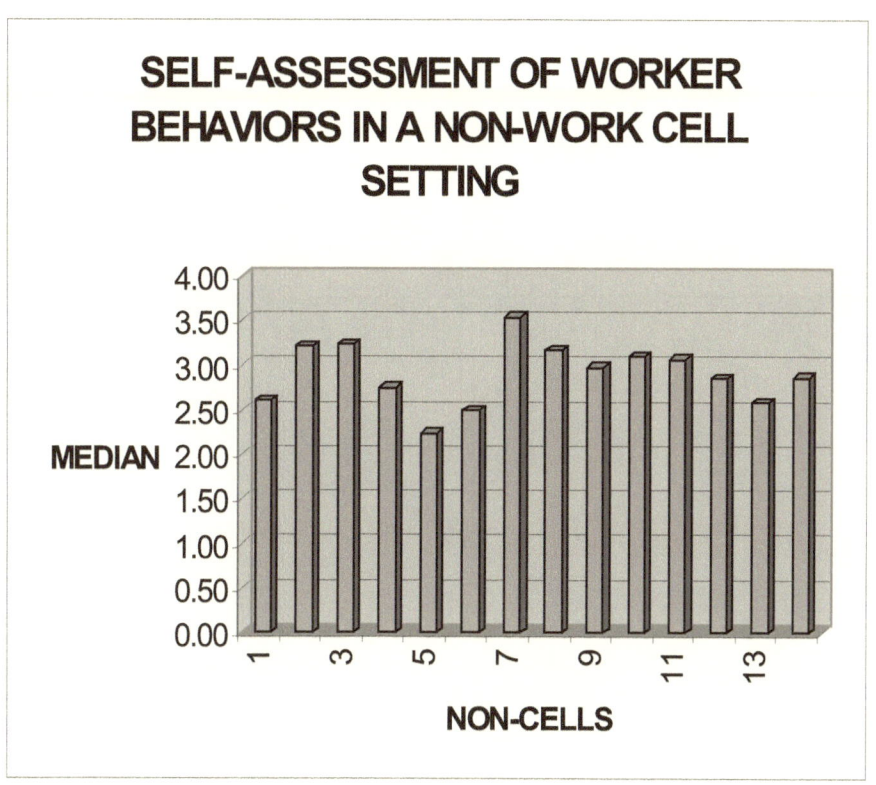

NON-WORK CELLS DEPARTMENT #272

Integrity of others, dignity/respect, and caring about others/business. It seems that personal growth/learning continues, and teamwork and winning were acceptable. Conversely, leadership is shared, accountability for work/behavior, empowerment, "we act in harmony," and "we accept personal responsibility" were the weakest.

Chapter 7

CONCLUSION AND RECOMMENDATIONS

Of all the problems and challenges faced in successfully implementing self-directed work teams, overcoming resistance to change is probably the single greatest barrier. Resistance to change is natural. Leaders who truly understand the reasons behind the human experience of resistance to change can more effectively reduce that "natural" resistance and facilitate the change process. Some of the reasons behind resistance to change are:

- Fear – Change means doing things differently and results in risk and the loss of a person's comfort zone

- Skepticism – Some change initiatives lack clear and obvious management commitment. No one wants to get geared up for a new way of working only to find out that management changed its mind or that it was just a passing fad

- No perceived need – Why are we doing this? We are doing just fine. What is the need? What are the benefits?

These are some of the resistance results from the Organizational Guiding Behavior Survey.

Conclusions

The pressure to perform will be more real than ever in the new work environment. The work climate is more relaxed because it fosters the spirit of cooperation. Cooperation builds on trust, a psychological factor, which has broad economic implications. Workers love to come to work. Group enterprise is fun. A self-directed work team is now a group phenomenon. "Two heads are better than one," and "working together is more fun than working alone," are part of the new vocabulary. Everyone is selling. This is the new reality: they are selling not as vendors, but selling as workers who have the best interests of their co-workers and the company at heart. The norm drives performance, giving the individual worker the incentive to help others to perform well, assuring the collective success of all.

Policy Recommendations

Self-directed work teams require a change in management's style of communication. The old management style of telling and not trusting associates now makes a 180-degree turn. Management has to become coaches and not authoritarians.

The coaching process is one of sitting down with the associates and truly listening to their concerns, fears, and points of view about the change process. In some cases, they just need to know that management has really heard their concerns. Think of this as the opportunity for them to "get it off their chest" that they did not feel they had in a group setting. At this stage, the leader's only job is to listen with compassion and understanding. Often, that is all it takes for these associates to move past their concerns and get on with the change process.

The next step in the coaching process is to again restate the situation the company is facing and the opportunity that self-directed teams offer. Then ask directly for their support and help. By asking, rather than demanding or threatening as in the command-and-control leadership style, the manager gives the team the choice to finally support the process or not.

If coaching efforts fail, then an alternative is to reassign the individual to a part of the company, or another division, that will be less directly affected by the change process. Sometimes this is a good win-win outcome where the knowledge and expertise of the individual can be retained, and the pathway cleared of resistance.

Recommendations for Further Research

Management at all levels within the organization should not be a bystander or a victim during these times of change. Whether or not the organization is actively addressing its culture or leadership issues, "you can make a difference." Everyone influences the cultural around them, be it in their organization, their department, or their work team. Each of us casts a shadow by his own behaviors, and each of us has a choice in teams of our own personal and professional development.

In addition, organizational transformation does not take place without personal transformation. If everyone waits for those above or around him or her to change, no one changes. This is the time when each individual needs to look at him or herself and decide ways in which he needs to change in order to more effectively deal with the changing times.

For further research on self-directed work teams, in addition to the references in this book, the Columbus Library and the Internet have additional information on these rapid workplace changes in progress.

Chapter 8

REFLECTION

Reflection on writing this book gives me a clearer insight into the need for business operations to change in today's work environment. The cited references provided documentation to show that a number of companies were able to maintain a competitive edge by making the transformation to self-directed work teams.

The increase in both U.S. and global competition has required firms to become innovative and incorporate ideas that increase associates' motivation and productivity while decreasing costs. One method that has had great success is the use of self-directed work teams. Self-directed work teams are increasing in their popularity, and many U.S. firms are using different forms of these teams to help increase production, streamline the organizational process, and maintain a higher level of commitment and motivation among associates.

I learned that the concept of self-directed work teams originated from the use of action teams. While both action teams and self-directed teams are good at increasing associates' confidence and development on individual bases, they differ in that action teams are formed to solve a specific problem within the company, while self-directed teams are given the task of undertaking full responsibility for an entire function of the company. Some of the functions self-directed work teams might be assigned to control include coordinating training, setting up schedules, budget responsibilities, disciplinary problems, and hiring practices.

The firm must follow its core values and goals. I learned that successful teams are found in organizations that believe in true empowerment and equality in the workforce. Companies that rely heavily on an autocratic system will have a difficult time gaining associates' acceptance for such an operation. Associates in this type of organization know there is no true empowerment and do not feel the need to put forth the extra effort needed to make a self-directed work team successful.

Once the decision is made that a self-directed work team would be beneficial to the company, the real work begins. It is not an easy process to develop a team. A great deal of time, patience, and resources are required of the team in order to have a successful beginning. Many times organizations rush into the formation of these teams, expecting results in unrealistic time periods. This only leads to frustration, both from upper management and from the associates involved in the process.

One important part of the formation of a self-directed work team, according to Dean Elmuti in his article "Sustaining High Performance Though Self-Managed Work Teams," is the link it has with empowerment. Elmuti states that allowing the associates the ability to make decisions that affect them is crucial to the success of the team. Empowerment is a good catchall phrase for today's business practice. It should not just be preached in order to obtain increases in individual motivation and

productivity.

Tom H. Washington

References

Barker, J. R. "Tightening the iron cage: Concretive control in self-managing teams." *Administrative Science Quarterly*, 1993a.

Barker, J. R. and Tompkins, P. K. *Identification in the Self-Managing organization: Human communication research*. [publisher missing here?], 1994.

Childress, John R. and Senn, Larry E. *In the Eye of the Storm: Reengineering Corporate Culture*. Los

Angeles/New York: The Leadership Press, August 1995.

Elmuti, Dean. "Sustaining High Performances Through Self-Managed Work Teams." *Industrial Management*, Mar/Apr 1996, Vol. 38, Issue 2, p. 4.

Glorioso, John E. "TQM and the Team Solution." *Security Management*, Oct 1994, Vol. 38, Issue 10, p. 33.

Kelly, Mark. *The Adventures of a Self-Management Team*, [publisher missing here?], 1991.

Passmore, William A. "Developing Self-Managing Work Teams: An Approach to Successful Integration."

Compensation and Benefits Review, Jul/Aug 1994, Vol. 26, Issue 4, p. 15.

Sundstrom, E., De Meuse, K., and Futrell, D. "Work teams: Applications and effectiveness." *American Psychologist*, [month?] 1990.

Weisbord, Marvin R. *Productive Workplaces: Organization and Managing for Dignity, Meaning, and Community*. San Francisco: Jossey-Bass Publishers, 1987.

Yeatts, Dale E., Hipskind, Martha, Barnes, Deborah. "Lessons Learned from Self-managed Work Teams." *Business Horizons*, Jul/Aug 1994, Vol. 37, p. 11.

Tom H. Washington

[author and title of article missing here?] *Futurist,*

Sep/Oct 1994, Vol. 28 Issue 5, pp. 48-50.

APPENDIX A

Problem Analysis Worksheet

1. Company is going to a self-directed work team environment.

2. Associates are reluctant to change. (Location of the problem is the production areas. All production departments are affected by the changes.)

1. **Description of current status:**	2. **Description of desired status:**
(a) Old style of management	(a) Self-directed work teams
(b) Lack of training	(b) Training for associates
(c) Lack of ownership	(c) Take ownership of the business
(d) Closed communication	(d) Open communication
(e) Lack of cross-training	(e) Cross-training
(f) Lack of leadership skills	(f) Training in leadership skills

4.SYMPTOMS	POSSIBLE CAUSE
Negative attitude	Lack of training
Reluctant to change	

5. **List of possible explanations:**

a Top management does not provide proper training for the associates to be effective at the new system

b Some supervisors are not ready to give up some of the authority in their given departments

c Supervisors are lacking training to be coaches in the self-directed work team system

d Ownership is lacking from some top managers in the area of self-directed work teams

e Our company has made the decision to go to self-directed teams, and I feel it is the duty of top management to make sure all associates, including management staff, get adequate training.

f   All points in line #6 and above are relevant for us to be successful in a self-directed work team environment, in my opinion.